Simply Movies

Music from the Silver Screen
20 Memorable Melodies
Arranged by Dan Coates

Simply Movies is a collection of the most famous songs and themes from the world's greatest films. These have been carefully selected and arranged by Dan Coates for Easy Piano, making many of cinema's most recognizable melodies accessible to pianists of all ages. Phrase markings, articulations, fingering and dynamics have been included to aid with interpretation, and a large print size makes the notation easy to read.

Many talented composers—including John Williams, Alan Menken, Howard Shore, Harold Arlen, Henry Mancini and many others—have written scores for motion pictures. Their music has provided tender backdrops for romances, exciting backgrounds for action sequences, reflections of characters' inner feelings, and swinging rhythms for some of the best dance numbers. When we think of Rocky Balboa training on the streets of Philadelphia, Superman flying over the skyscrapers of Metropolis, or Dorothy journeying along the yellow brick road, we think of the music that accompanied them. This music, with its spirit and charm, has been embraced by musicians and audiences, young and old, around the world. For these reasons and more, this music is exciting to explore.

After all, it is *Simply Movies!*

Contents

The Colors of the Wind

from *Walt Disney's "Pocahontas"*

Lyrics by Stephen Schwartz
Music by Alan Menken
Arranged by Dan Coates

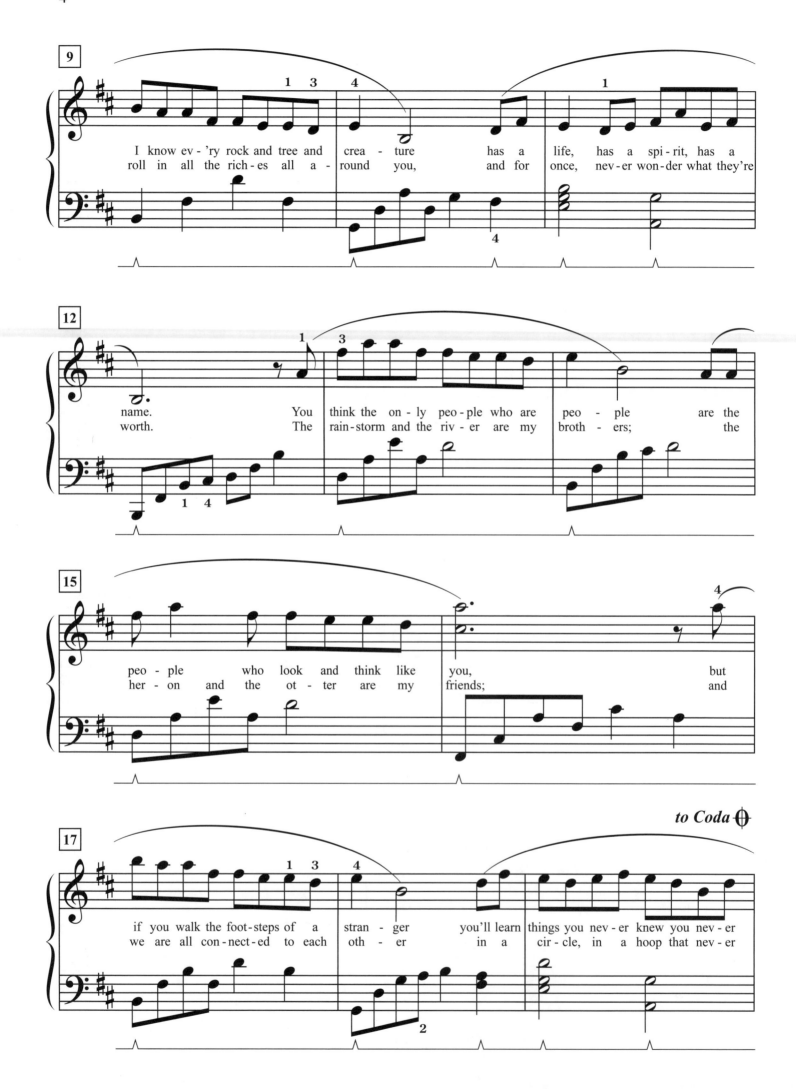

Adelieland

from *Happy Feet*

Composed by John Powell
Arranged by Dan Coates

Bright Latin beat

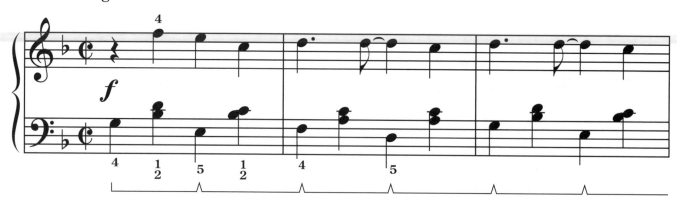

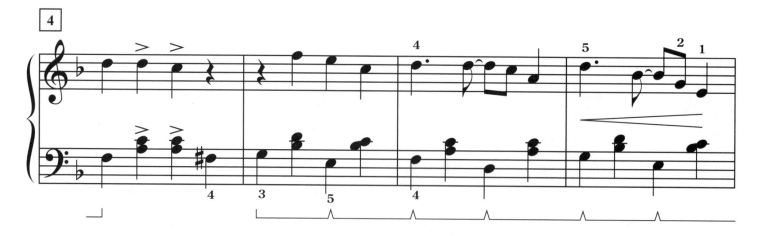

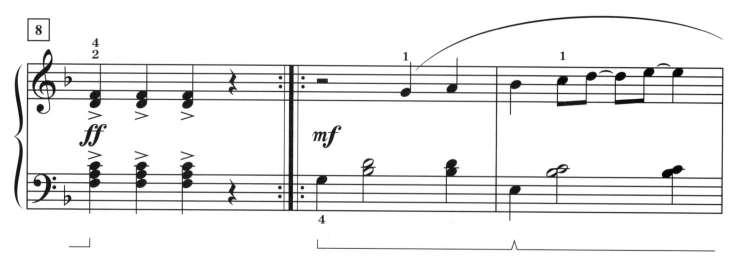

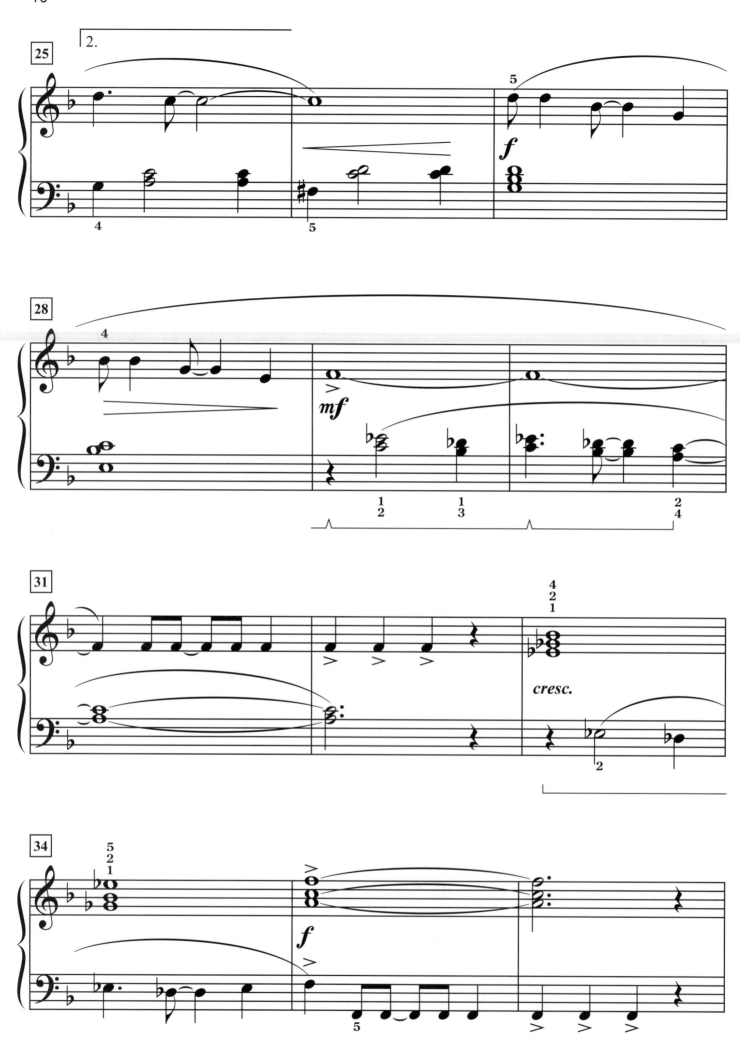

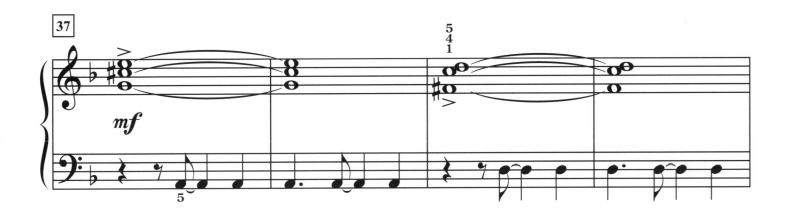

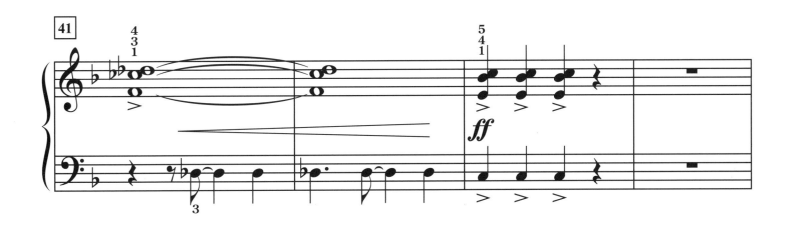

And All That Jazz
from *Chicago*

Lyrics by Fred Ebb
Music by John Kander
Arranged by Dan Coates

Start the car,— I know a whoop - ee spot— where the gin is cold but the pi -
Hold on, hon,— we're gon - na bun - ny hug,— I bought some as - pi - rin— down at U -

an - o's hot.— It's just a nois - y hall— where there's a night - ly brawl— and
nit - ed Drug— in case we shake a - part— and want a brand new start— to

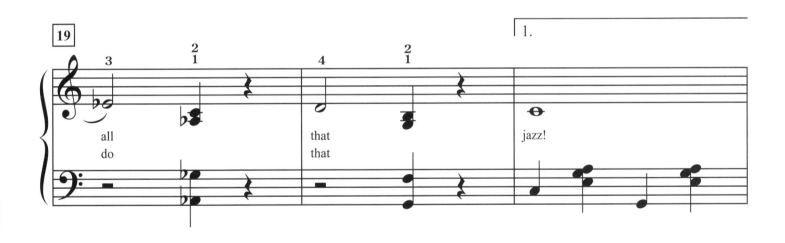

1.

all
do
that that jazz!

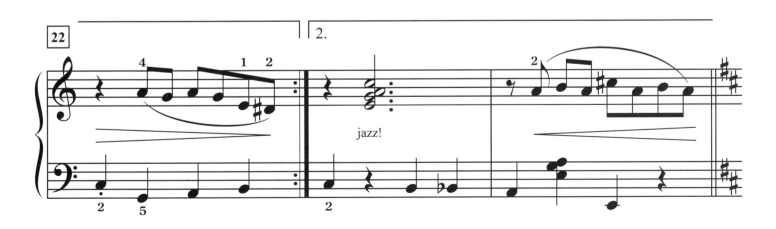

2.

jazz!

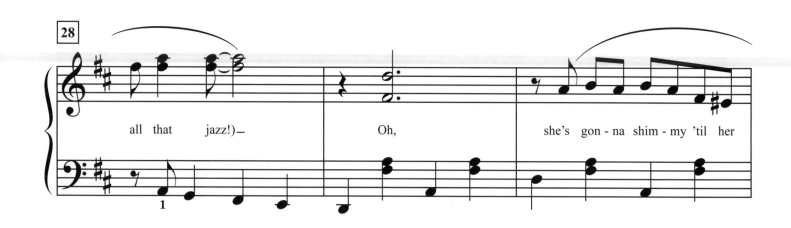

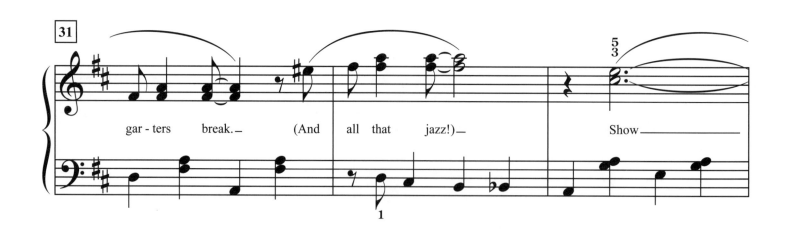

if she'd hear— her ba-by's queer— for all

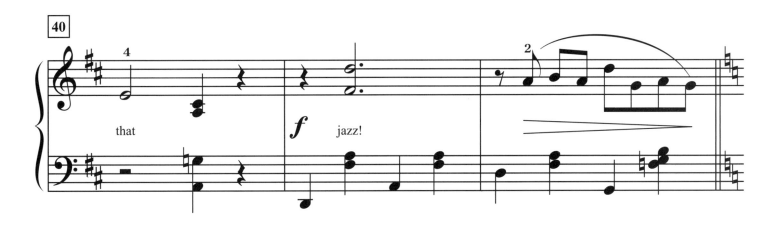

that *f* jazz!

Find a flask,— we're play-ing fast and loose— and all that jazz!—

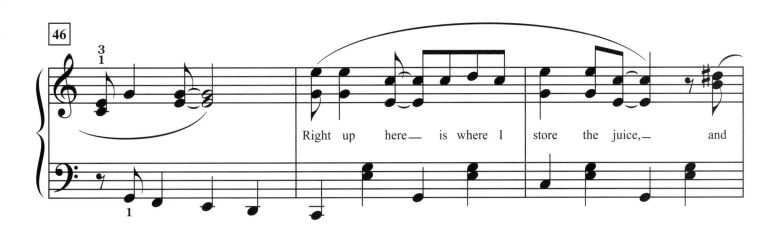

Right up here— is where I store the juice,— and

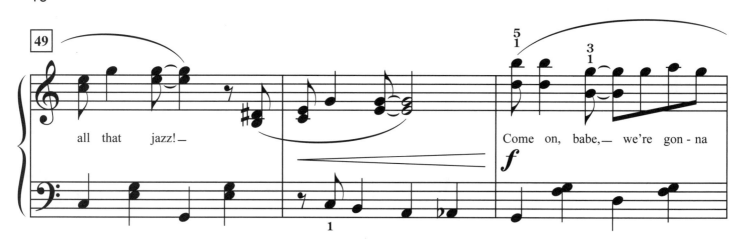

all that jazz!— Come on, babe,— we're gon-na

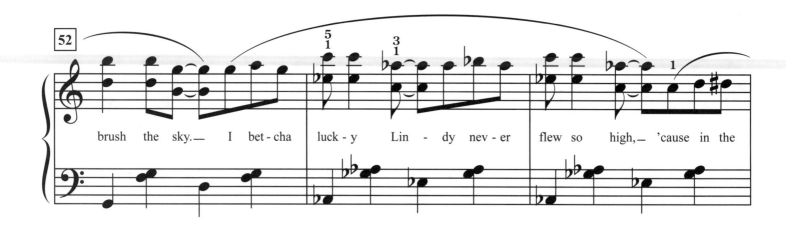

brush the sky.— I bet-cha luck-y Lin - dy nev-er flew so high,— 'cause in the

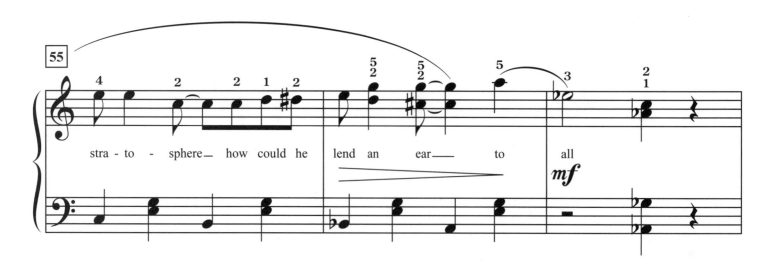

stra-to-sphere— how could he lend an ear— to all

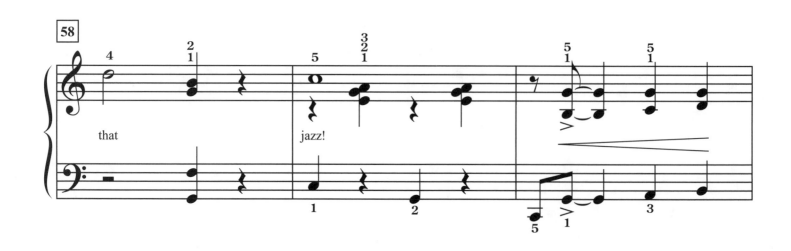

that jazz!

As Time Goes By

from *Casablanca*

Words and Music by
Herman Hupfeld
Arranged by Dan Coates

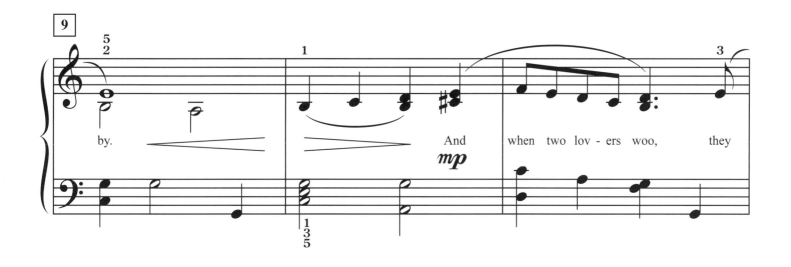

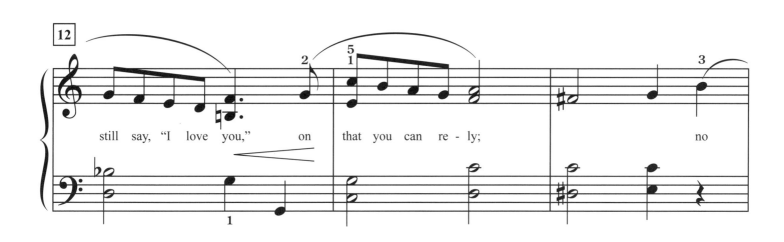

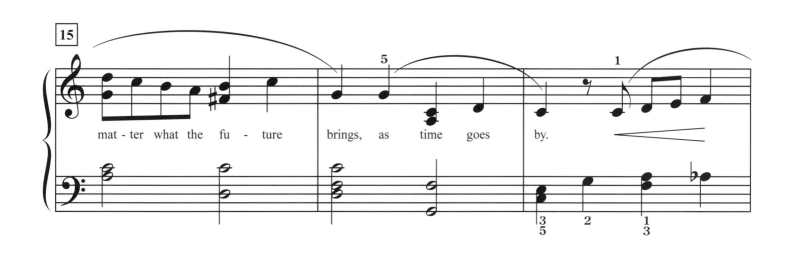

Moon - light and love songs nev - er out of date,

mf

hearts full of pas - sion, jeal - ou - sy and hate; wom - an needs man and

f

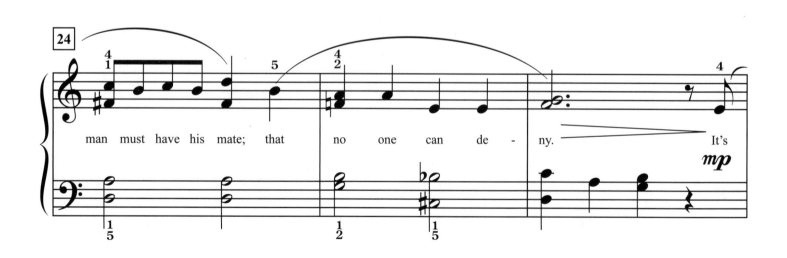

man must have his mate; that no one can de - ny. It's

mp

still the same old sto - ry, a fight for love and glo - ry, a case of do or die!

The world will al - ways wel - come lov - ers, as

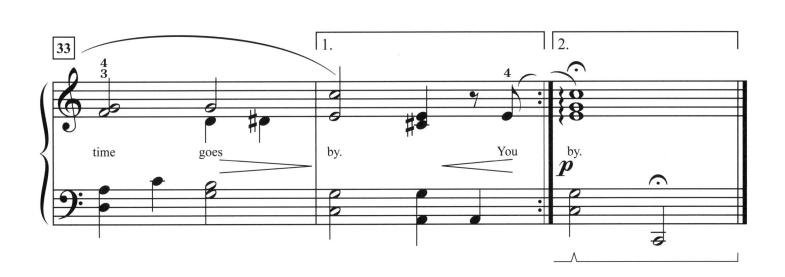

time goes by. You by.

Beauty and the Beast

from *Walt Disney's "Beauty and the Beast"*

Music by Alan Menken
Lyrics by Howard Ashman
Arranged by Dan Coates

Slowly, with expression

Corpse Bride (Main Title)

Music by Danny Elfman
Arranged by Dan Coates

The Departed Tango

from *The Departed*

By Howard Shore
Arranged by Dan Coates

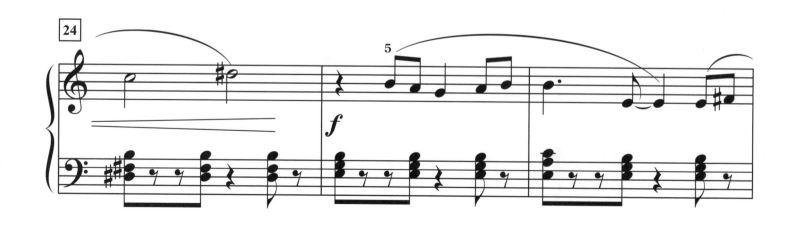

Gonna Fly Now
Theme from *Rocky*

Words and Music by Bill Conti,
Ayn Robbins and Carol Connors
Arranged by Dan Coates

With a steady, driving beat

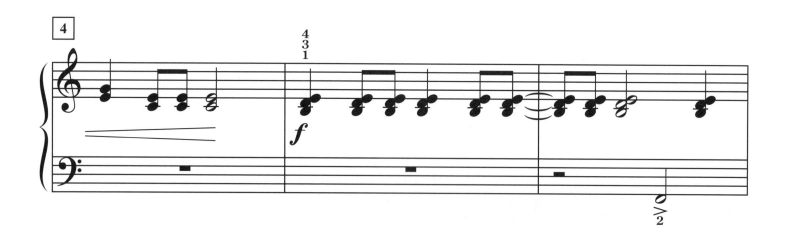

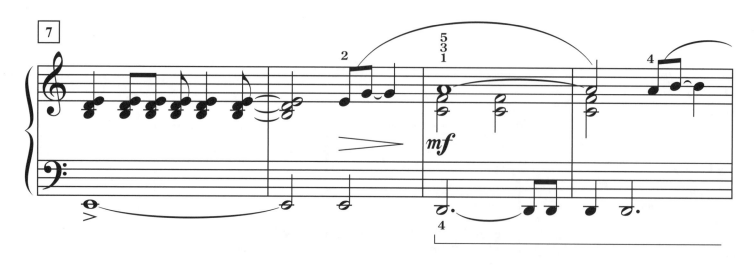

If I Only Had a Brain

from *The Wizard of Oz*

Music by Harold Arlen
Lyric by E.Y. Harburg
Arranged by Dan Coates

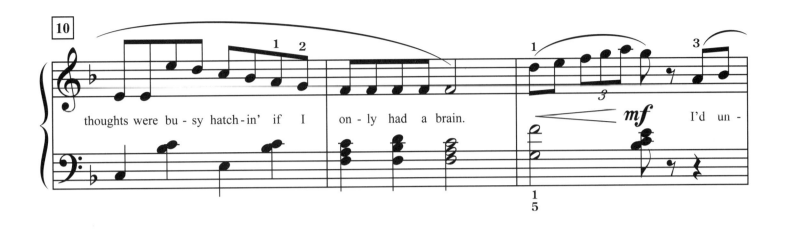

thoughts were bu - sy hatch-in' if I on - ly had a brain. I'd un -

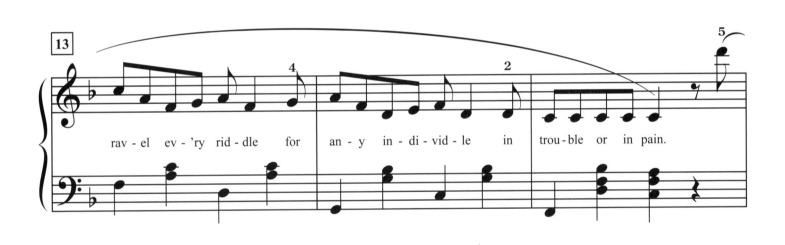

rav - el ev - 'ry rid - dle for an - y in - di - vid - le in trou - ble or in pain.

With the thoughts I'd be think-in' I could be an - oth - er Lin - coln, if I

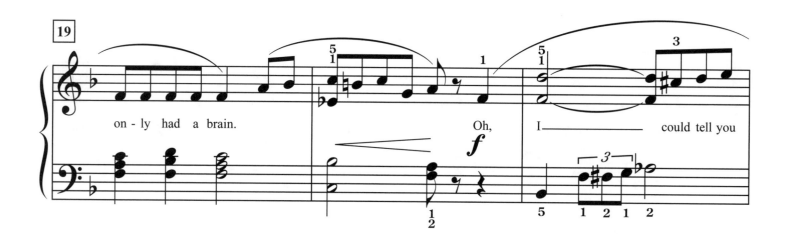

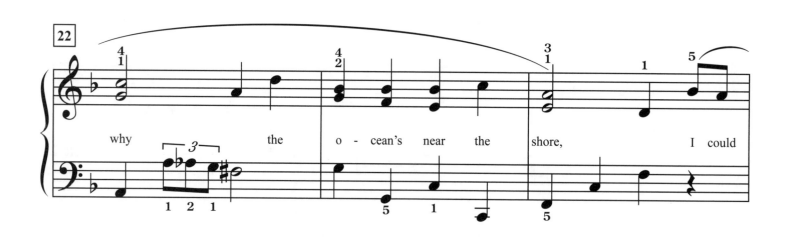

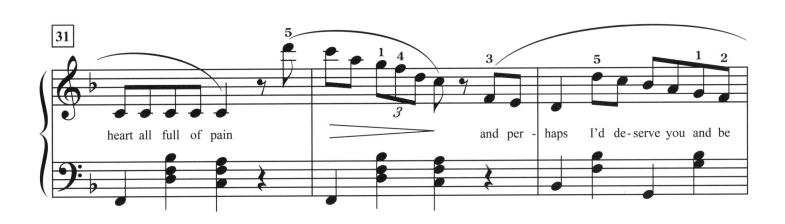

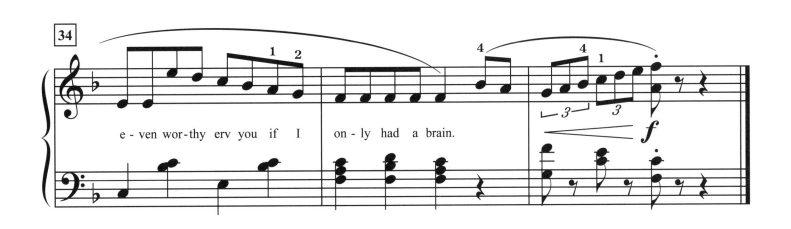

James Bond Theme

By Monty Norman
Arranged by Dan Coates

Moderately bright

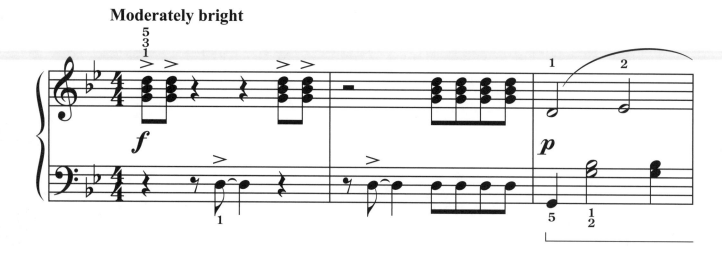

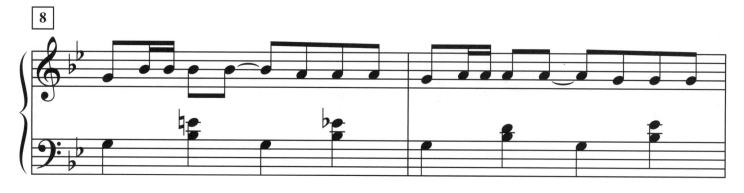

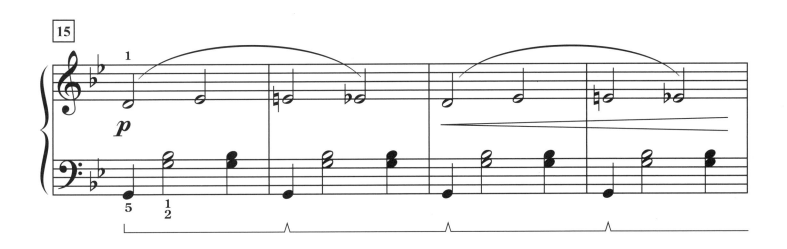

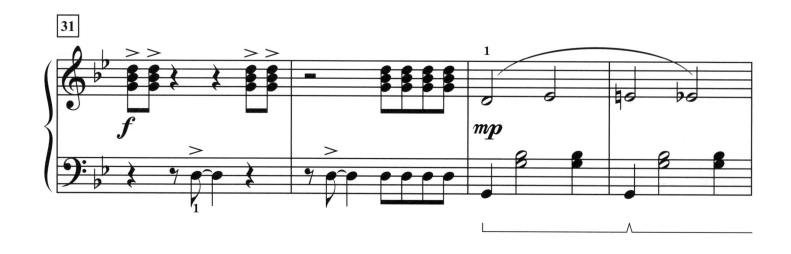

The Notebook (Main Title)

Words and Music by
Aaron Zigman
Arranged by Dan Coates

Slowly, with expression

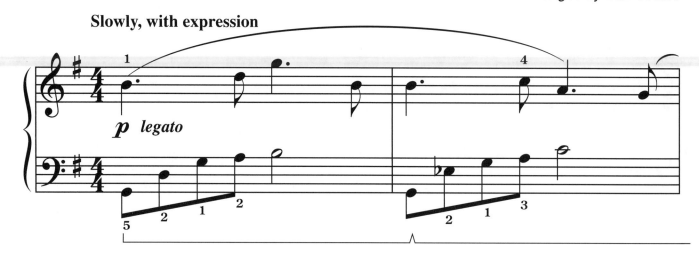

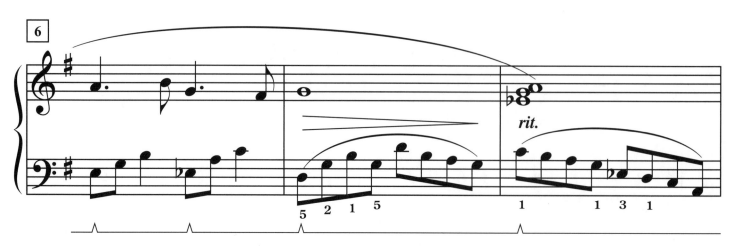

Over the Rainbow

from *The Wizard of Oz*

Music by Harold Arlen
Lyric by E.Y. Harburg
Arranged by Dan Coates

The Pink Panther

By Henry Mancini
Arranged by Dan Coates

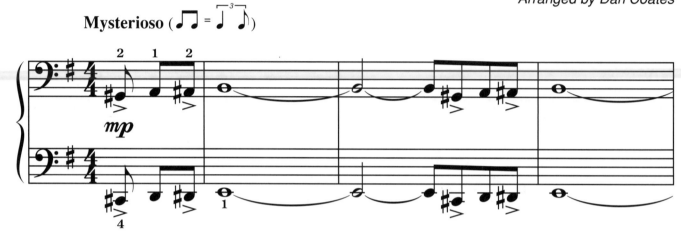

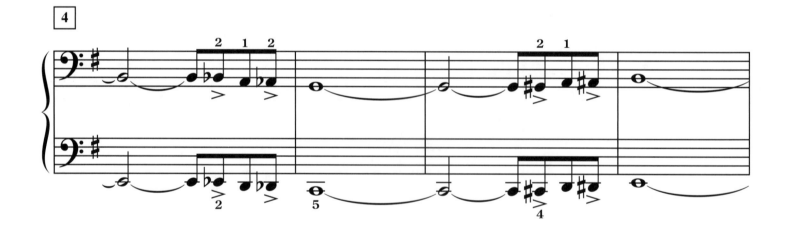

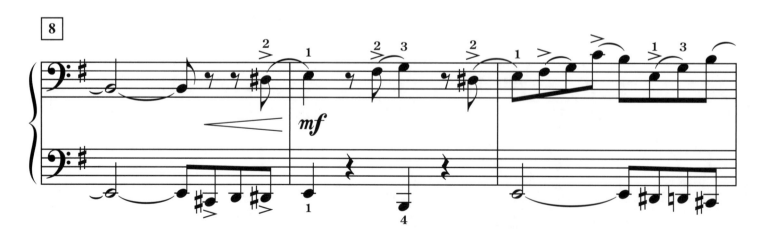

54

The Rose

Words and Music by
Amanda McBroom
Arranged by Dan Coates

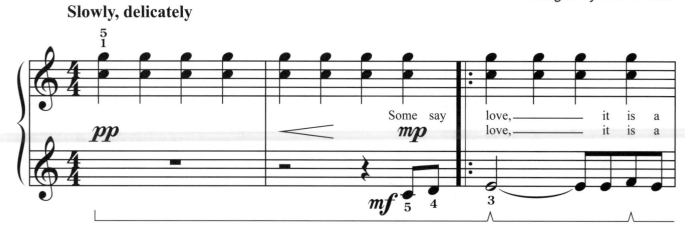

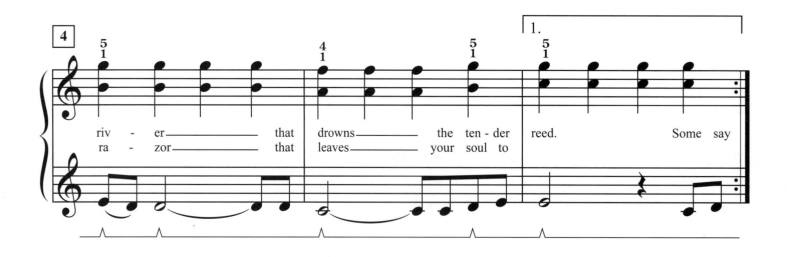

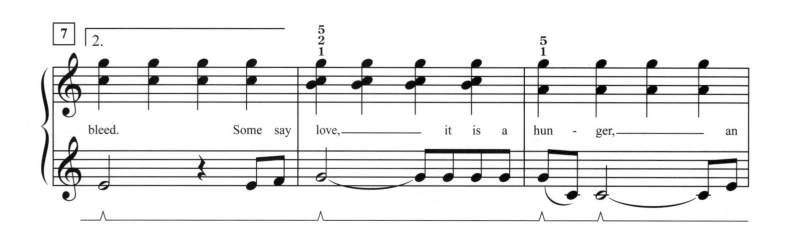

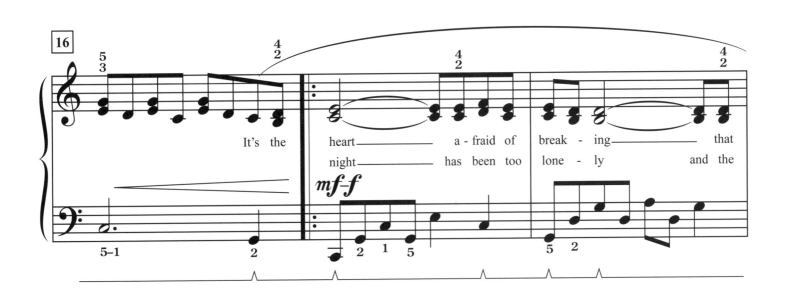

give,————— and the soul————— a-fraid of dy—ing————— that
snows————— lies the seed————— that with the sun's— love in the

mp

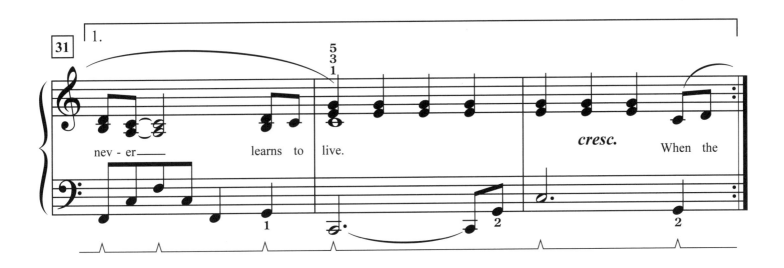

1.

nev - er———— learns to live. *cresc.* When the

2.

a tempo

spring———— be-comes the rose. *rit.*

rit. *p*

8va

In Dreams
from *The Lord of the Rings*

Words and Music by
Fran Walsh and Howard Shore
Arranged by Dan Coates

29

rit. When the

32 *a tempo*

seas and moun - tains fall and we come to end of

35

days,———— in the dark I hear a call, call - ing me

38

there. I will go there——— and back a - gain.———

rit.

p

Singin' in the Rain

Music by Nacio Herb Brown
Lyric by Arthur Freed
Arranged by Dan Coates

Star Wars (Main Title)

By **JOHN WILLIAMS**
Arranged by Dan Coates

Theme from "Superman"

By **JOHN WILLIAMS**
Arranged by Dan Coates

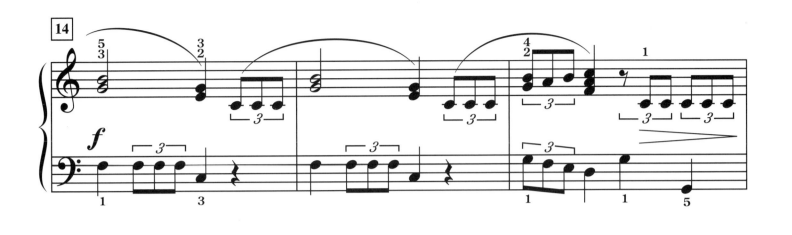

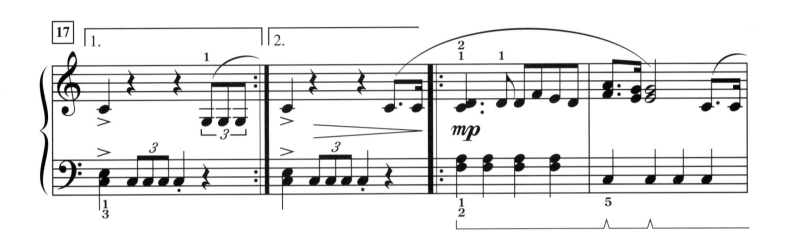

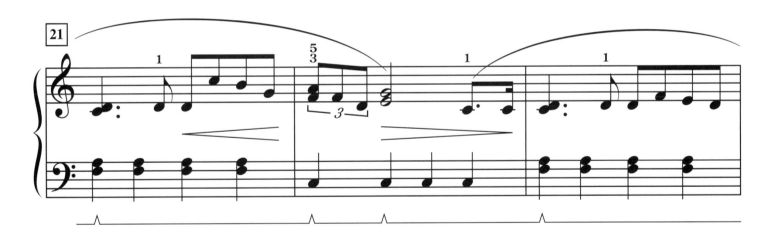

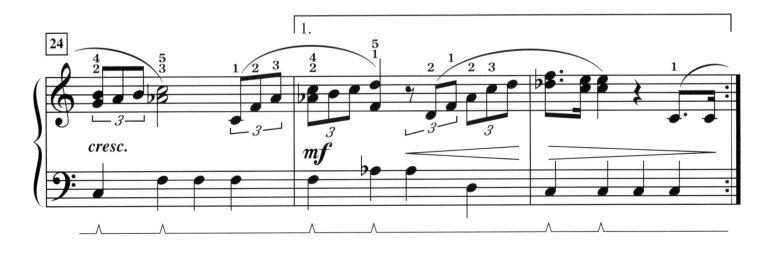

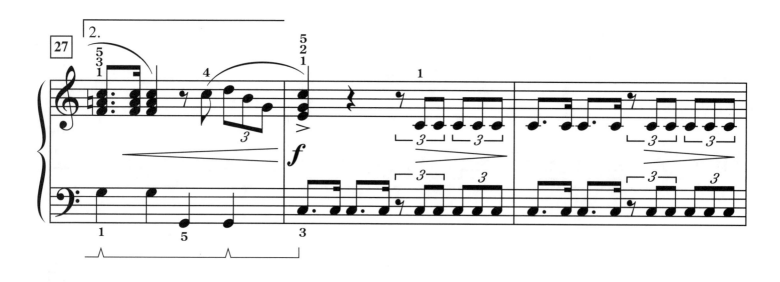

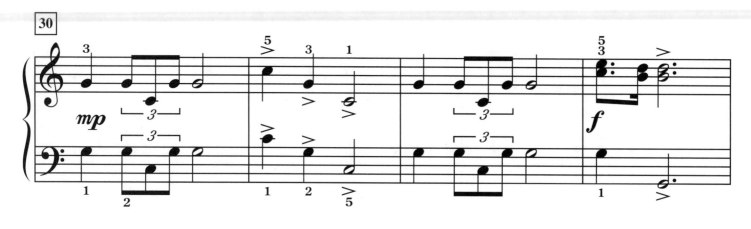

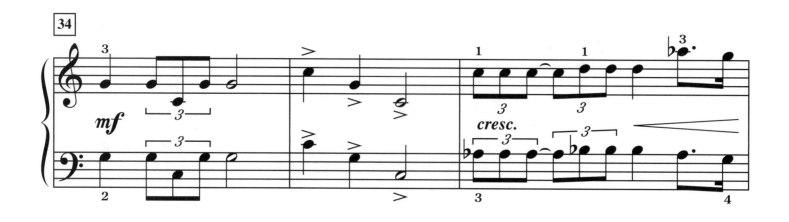

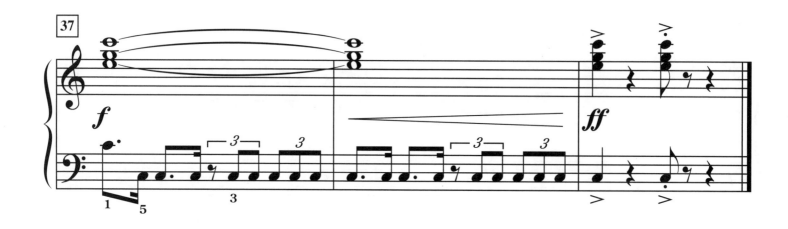

The Wind Beneath My Wings

from *Beaches*

Words and Music by
Larry Henley and Jeff Silbar
Arranged by Dan Coates

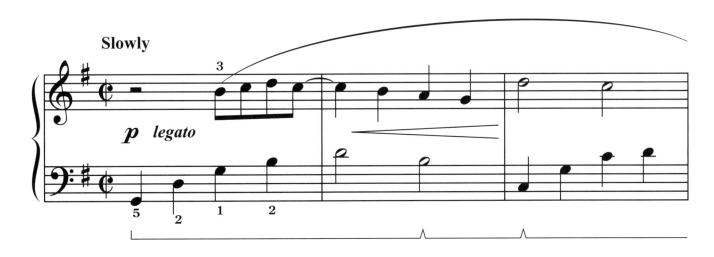

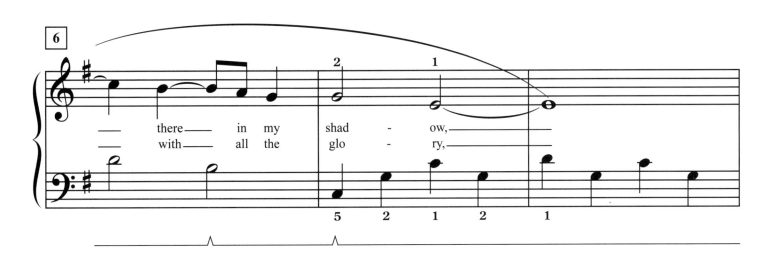

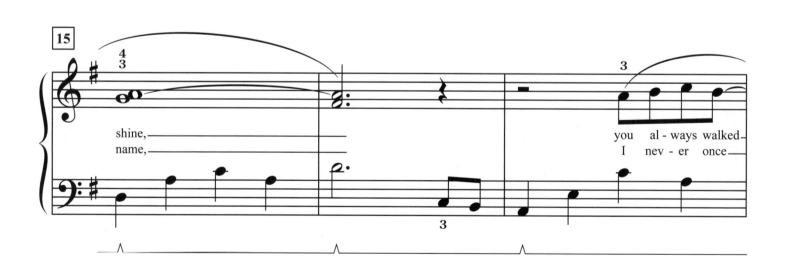

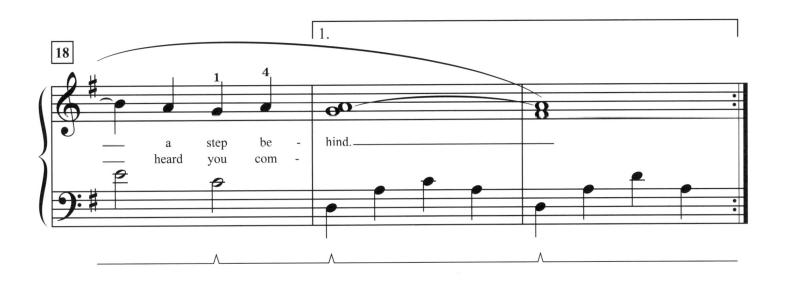

a step be - hind.
heard you com -

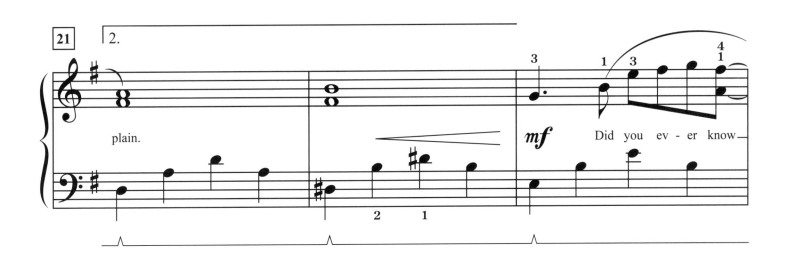

plain.

mf Did you ev - er know

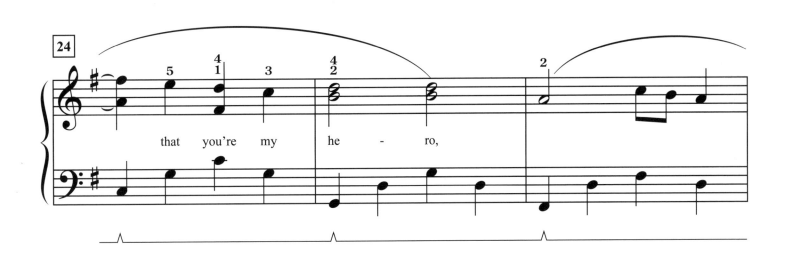

that you're my he - ro,

and ev - 'ry - thing___ I'd like to be?

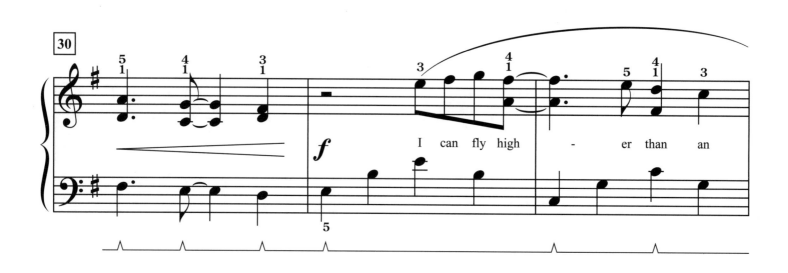

I can fly high - er than an

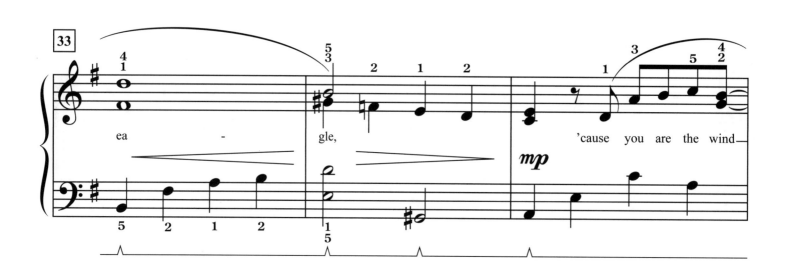

ea - gle, 'cause you are the wind___

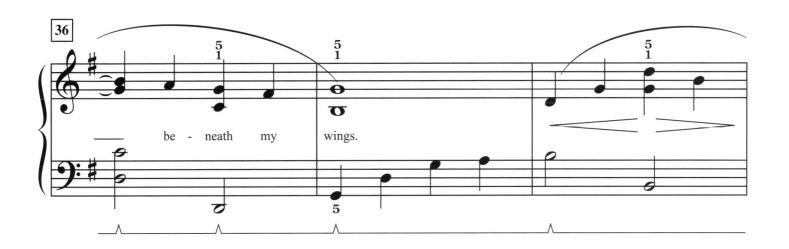

be - neath my wings.

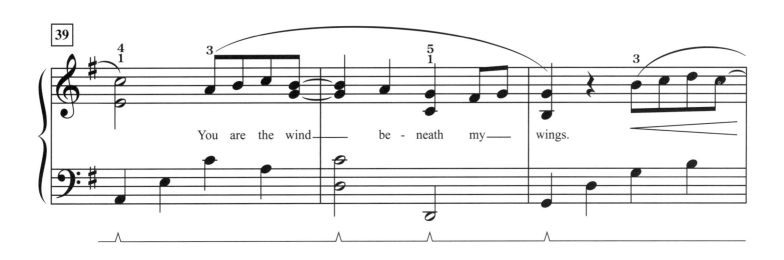

You are the wind be - neath my wings.

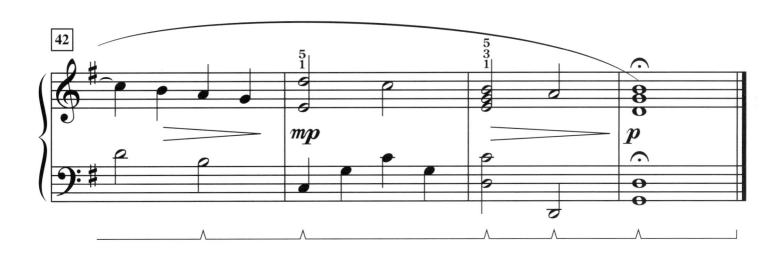

A Whole New World

from *Walt Disney's "Aladdin"*

Words by Time Rice
Music by Alan Menken
Arranged by Dan Coates

Moderately, with expression

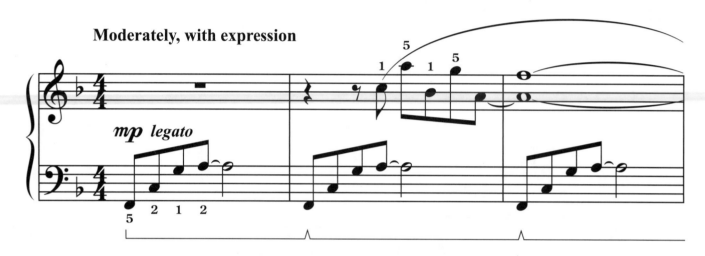

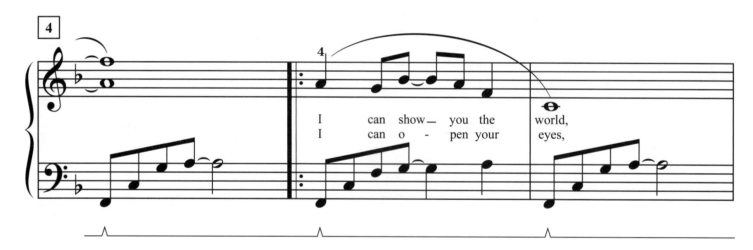

I can show— you the world,
I can o - pen your eyes,

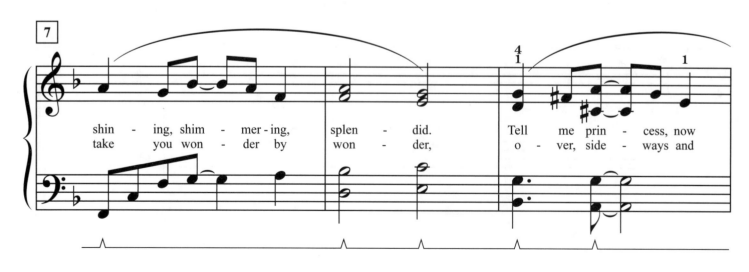

shin - ing, shim - mer - ing, splen - did. Tell me prin - cess, now
take you won - der by won - der, o - ver, side - ways and

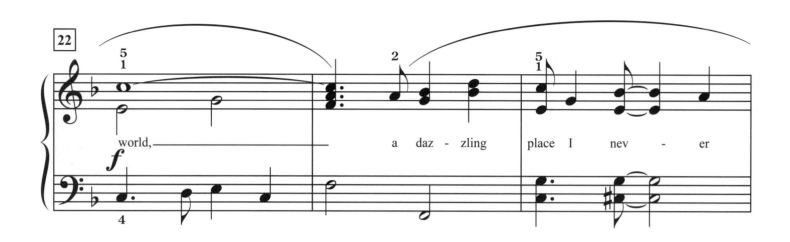

world,_____ a daz - zling place I nev - er

knew. But when I'm way up here it's cry - stal clear that

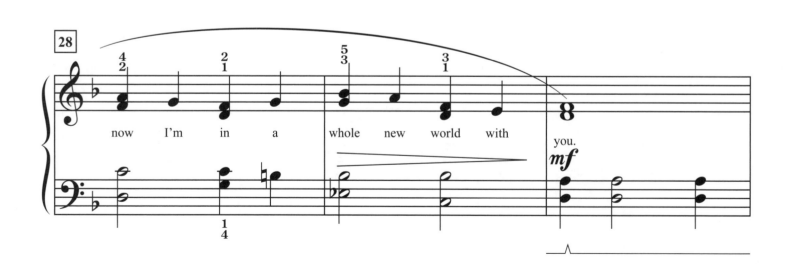

now I'm in a whole new world with you.

31 A whole new world, that's where we'll

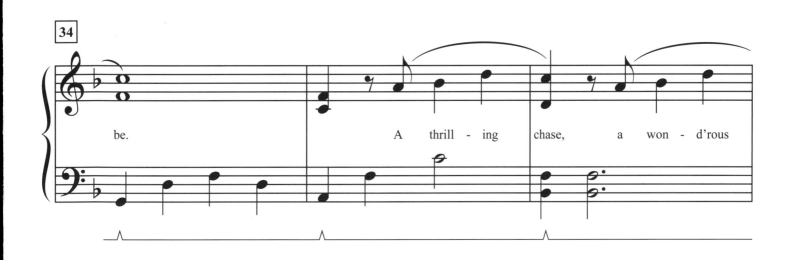

34 be. A thrill - ing chase, a won - d'rous

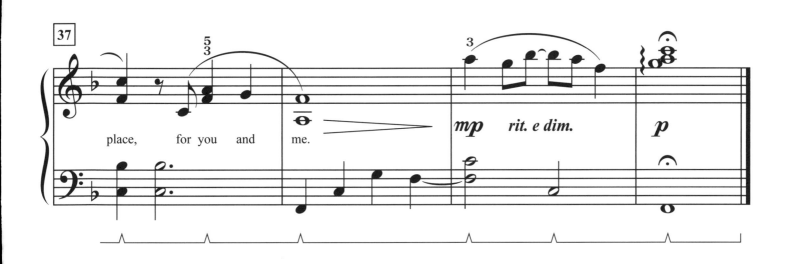

37 place, for you and me. *mp rit. e dim. p*